JOSH DISCOVERS PASSOVER!

Written by Larry Stein

Illustrated by Marlene K. Goodman

Ruach Publishing

Deerfield, Illinois

Long ago, Passover was not exactly one of my favorite holidays.
The Seders were *sooo* long and I couldn't even eat bagels!
Then, in one incredible night, things changed for me.
Now, I'm crazy about Passover! I love it!
Here's how it all began:
My Uncle walked in the house, carrying a box.
I knew that was trouble... big trouble.

Matzah: the bread of both slavery and freedom.
There are two sides to matzah. Since we ate matzah as slaves, eating it on Passover reminds us to be humble. Matzah is also the bread of freedom, since we ate it after we were freed from Egypt. I like eating matzah on Passover, but I *really* miss my bagels!

My uncle opened the box and my Mom gasped:
"Josh, it's your great-grandfather's *tallit*! Try it on!"
I smiled politely, "Uh, that's okay, maybe later..."
Then I felt a big hand on my shoulder – my Dad's.
That was it. Now I'd have to try it on.
Sometimes it's *really* lousy being a kid.

What's so important about the *tzitzit* (fringes) of a *tallit*?
a) They're kinda cool, Israeli rock singers wear 'em.
b) They were history's first fashion statement.
c) They're a symbol of God's 613 commandments.
d) Actually, the stripes are much more important.
Careful: some questions have 2 or more answers!
See answers on pages 30-31.

3

My Uncle wrapped the *tallit* around my shoulders.
Suddenly, the room began to spin!
Then I began to spin!
History flashed before my eyes.
My Mom's voice grew faint, "Josh? Joshy?"
Soon, I stopped spinning and couldn't hear her at all.

Passover dates back more than 3000 years!
I saw a lot of Jewish history! The Israelites left Egypt more than 3000 years ago, around 1250 B.C.E. Later, Moses received the Torah, which includes the story of Passover. After thousands of years, we still read the Torah at least three days every week!

I found myself dressed in robes, knee-deep in mud!
There were thousands like me, making bricks.
I couldn't believe it: I was a slave in Egypt!
It was awful! What did I do to deserve this?
We worked all day, with no time for rest or play –
no baseball, no TV, no computer... no nothing!

Which food reminds us of slaves making bricks?
a) Tongue (*our tongues hung out from exhaustion*)
b) Matzah (*our backs had gashes from the whips*)
c) Shankbone (*we were worked to the bone*)
d) Charoset (*it looks like the mortar used for bricks*)

Within hours, I ached all over from the hard work.
I was in such pain, I could barely move.
A guard yelled, "Back to work, slave!"
And he slashed his whip across my back.
"Owwwwch!" I fell face first into the mud.
Then, a big hand reached down to pull me up.
I looked up. Could it be? Yes... it was Moses!

How long were our ancestors slaves in Egypt?
a) 40 hours (*that's why we work 40-hour weeks!*)
b) 40 days
c) 40 years
d) 400 years

Moses led me out of the mudpits toward his house.
Suddenly, we saw an Egyptian whipping a slave.
Moses called out, "Let him go!"
Quickly, Moses moved in to help the slave.
But in doing so, the Egyptian lost his life.
It was very, very sad.

Passover teaches us to be kind to everyone.
The experience of the Jewish people as slaves in Egypt
should teach us to be kind and caring toward everyone,
since our ancestors were once "strangers in a strange land."
In fact, it's a *mitzvah* to invite those who are hungry or in
need to join you at your Passover Seder table.

After that, Moses knew he had to leave Egypt.
He set off into the desert.
I worried about him. How could he survive?
The sun was hot and there was no food or water.
So, I ran in after him and we walked together.
Oh boy, was that a mistake! It was *sooo* hot!

Next time, I'll think about going into the desert!
Deserts are super hot, often over 100 degrees!
Now that's hot! Like bagels baking in an oven.
Oh no, now I miss my bagels even more!

We became shepherds and tended sheep.
It was pretty boring, but at least it wasn't the desert.
Then, one day, Moses looked out into the wilderness.
He pointed, "Look at that bush, it's amazing!
It keeps burning, yet its branches and leaves are still there!
You wait here, I want to take a closer look."

Many great leaders in the Bible were:
a) Rabbis
b) Shepherds
c) Astronauts
d) Camel racers

9

Moses returned after awhile, struck with awe.

"God told me to go to Egypt to free our people."

"*Whaaat?*" I gasped. "*God* spoke to you?"

Moses nodded, yes. I cried out, "You can't go back
to Egypt – they'll arrest you... or worse!
And how can we free our people without an army?"

"We don't need an army," said Moses,
 "God will help."

**When first told by God
to help free the Israelites, Moses replied:**
a) "Who me? Why would they listen to me?"
b) "What will I say when they ask Your name?"
c) "Yes, I will lead them to freedom."
d) Moses didn't say anything, he simply bowed.

We went with Moses' brother, Aaron, to see Pharaoh.
The palace was big and scary, and filled with armed guards.
Moses stated, "God said to let My people go."
Pharaoh laughed, "What God? Who is this God? No, Moses,
I won't let your people go. In fact, I'll make them work even harder!"

Pharaoh couldn't understand a God he couldn't see.
The Egyptians worshiped idols, like statues of animals.
Pharaoh even thought he was a god to be worshiped!
Maybe that's why it took all ten plagues before Pharaoh
freed the slaves. The plagues eventually led to the end
of idol worshiping and the widespread belief in one God.

So, Aaron threw down his rod. It turned into a snake!

Pharaoh laughed, "My magicians can do that!"

And they did.

But then, Aaron's snake ate Pharaoh's snakes!

Pharaoh said, "These tricks prove nothing.

No, I won't let your people go."

How did Pharaoh's magicians turn rods into snakes?
a) A super-secret Egyptian chant (I don't even know it!).
b) It's a trick from the Old Egyptian Magic Book, page 52.
c) They prayed to the rod god.
d) The rods were actually snakes, it wasn't magic at all.

With that, the plagues began.
Aaron struck the Nile River with his rod.
The river turned to blood! Yuk! Was that gross!
Soon, all of the waters in Egypt turned to blood!
The Egyptians couldn't drink water, wash or eat fish.
Moses asked, "Now will you let my people go?"
Pharaoh said yes at first, then refused to let us go.

The Nile was more than just a river to the Egyptians.
The Nile River was so important to the Egyptians that they worshiped it as a god! When the first plague struck the Nile River, it damaged a key source of Egypt's food and water, and also an idol. In the Passover story, we learn that we cannot worship idols, only the one true God.

13

More plagues hit the Egyptian people.
Frogs swarmed all over, hopping everywhere.
Bugs crawled over the Egyptians day and night.
Large beasts stampeded the area, smashing things.
And disease killed all of the Egyptians' cattle.
But after each plague, Pharaoh refused to let us go.

What did Pharaoh's magicians call the third plague, lice (bugs)?
a) The hand of Aaron
b) The fist of Moses
c) The finger of God
d) The foot in the mouth of Pharaoh

And so, more plagues struck the Egyptians.
Boils marked their skin, making them itch.
Hail stones pelted them wherever they went.
Locusts ruined their plants and crops.
And days of darkness made it impossible to see.
Again, after each terrible plague, Pharaoh said no.

The Ten Plagues also had an impact on the Israelites.
The Ten Plagues not only made life terribly difficult for the
Egyptians, they strengthened the Israelites' belief in God!
Today, miracles are less obvious than in Moses' time.
But if you look closely, you can see miracles every day
and our belief in God should be stronger than ever.

After the ninth plague, Pharaoh threatened Moses,
"I warn you, don't ever come here again."
"Okay, I won't see you anymore," Moses said,
"But there will be a terrible tenth plague:
it will destroy all of Egypt's first born!"
And Moses stormed out of the palace.

We still celebrate Jewish first-born males with a:
a) *Pidyon Habben* ceremony
b) Fast for the First Born (during *Erev Pesach*)
c) Feast of the First Pizza (after Pesach, of course)
d) Fight for the First Bagel (I always win this one!)

Moses returned to us and told all of the Israelites,
"Spread lamb's blood on your doorposts,
it will be a sign for God to *pass over* your homes."
I was smart – I put the blood on the door myself.
You see, I didn't want any slip-ups, I'm a first-born too!
I may not look like much right now, but someday,
the Cubs could really use me at shortstop!

The *mezuzah*: a meaningful sign on our doorposts.
Jewish people continue to put an important sign on the
doorposts of our homes (a *mezuzah*) to remind us of
God's presence in our lives. In fact, *mezuzah* is the
Hebrew word for doorpost.

After we spread the lamb's blood on the doorposts, we ate roasted lamb, matzah and maror at a big meal. I asked, "What is the meaning of this service?" Aaron replied, "To appreciate that God is saving us from the tenth plague and freeing us from slavery." Moses smiled, "Congratulations Josh, you just asked the first question of the first Passover Seder!"

We used to eat the *Pesach* on Pesach, but no longer!
So that's what *Pesach* means: it's the Passover sacrifice, the lamb we ate at the first Passover meal. We don't eat the *Pesach* (sacrifice) anymore, since we stopped sacrifices after the Second Temple was destroyed in 70 C.E. Today, the shankbone reminds us of the *Pesach*.

The tenth plague struck the Egyptians at midnight.
Later that night, Pharaoh called for Moses and Aaron.
When Moses and Aaron returned from the palace,
I heard the news and couldn't believe it,
"We're free? Really? We're leaving Egypt?
No more whips, no more slavery! Thank God!"

Midnight is important to Passover, it's when:
a) My Mom won't let me eat any more food.
b) The tenth plague struck the Egyptians.
c) We must have already eaten the *Afikoman*.
d) The Seder leader turns into a frog.

We packed up everything and hurried outside.
I stood with Moses in front of our people.
Shivers zoomed down my spine – it was like seeing
a big city full of people, all jammed in front of us!
A shofar blast rang through the crowd.
We set out to leave Egypt – we were really free!

We should appreciate God's gift of freedom.
Can you imagine your entire family as slaves, dating back
to your great, great, great, great grandparents, and more?
After about 400 years in Egypt, it was so great to be free!
Being free includes the freedom to live a Jewish life –
so do it! – and appreciate God's gift of freedom.

Days after leaving Egypt, we rested by the sea.
Suddenly, we heard the rumbling of Egyptian chariots!
We were trapped! The only way out was through
the sea, and that was impossible! But not to Moses.
He stretched his hand out over the water and
God sent a strong wind to part the sea!

Which sea did the Israelites cross?
a) The Red Sea
b) The Dead Sea
c) The Sea of Reeds
d) The See Ya Later Sea

Crossing the sea was incredible!
We walked on dry land between two walls of water!
As we crossed the sea, a cloud blocked the Egyptians.
But when we finally reached land, the cloud lifted.
Oh no! The Egyptians rushed in to attack! Now what?
It seemed hopeless! But not to Moses. He stretched
out his hand and God collapsed the walls of water!

How did Moses part the sea and cave it back in?
a) No big deal – they do it all the time in the movies.
b) He didn't – that sea moves in and out with the tides.
c) He didn't – it happens there every 18 years.
d) He didn't – it was all the work of God.

Finally, we were safe! What a great feeling... phew!
God led us through the desert to Mount Sinai,
with a cloud by day and a pillar of fire at night.
As we traveled, we built huts called *sukkot*.
And here's something really amazing:
manna rained from the sky to give us food!

Here's why we use two loaves of challah on Shabbat:
God sent a double portion of *manna* on Friday, so we wouldn't
have to work to gather food on Shabbat. Today, as a reminder of
the double portion, we recite the *Hamotzi* prayer over two loaves
of challah on Shabbat. In Hebrew, *manna* means: what is it?
The Israelites couldn't even describe it!

After a long trip, we finally reached Mount Sinai.
Moses stayed up on the mountain for forty days.
It was so long, our people began to lose faith.
Gold was melted and turned into a golden calf,
then worshiped like a god. It was terrible!
I tried to stop them, but they were out of control!

The gold used to make the golden calf was:
a) Found in the Great Gold Rush of 1250 B.C.E.
b) Bought from Sam the Jeweler (1-800-GoSammy).
c) Bought online at www.GottaLottaGold.com.
d) Given to our ancestors by the Egyptians.

At last, Moses appeared on a ridge of Mount Sinai.
He carried two stone tablets – the Ten Commandments.
But when Moses saw the golden calf and idol worshiping,
he became so angry that he threw down the stone tablets!
Then he smashed the golden calf!
I couldn't believe it! But I understood it:
we can only worship God, not idols.

The Torah has a lot more commandments than ten.
The Torah contains the Ten Commandments and a lot more –
613 commandments in all! God's 613 commandments tell us
how to live our lives, covering everything from what we eat
to how we should treat other people, and so much more.
In Hebrew, God's commandments are called *mitzvot*. 25

Soon after, Moses returned to Mount Sinai and received a second set of tablets written with the Ten Commandments. We wandered the desert for forty years, until we were finally ready to live by God's laws and enter the Promised Land, Israel. This was the best day of my life – we were finally free and we were about to step foot in Israel! We couldn't wait to get there!

God kept the covenant (promise), now how about us?
To reward Abraham's faithfulness, God promised that his descendants would live in the Promised Land. God kept that promise, now how about us? Are we being faithful and living up to God's commandments? Remember, God's covenant is both a gift and a responsibility.

As we entered Israel, I began to spin again. Uh oh!
I found myself at the Seder table. My sister, Leah, read:
"Why is this night different from all other nights?"
I smiled, "On this night, we remember how God brought
our people out of Egypt and led us to freedom."
Mom said, "Josh, that's not in the Four Questions."
I laughed, "Yeah, I know, you had to be there!"

Why do we celebrate Passover?
a) It's the law!
b) What else can you do with all that matzah?
c) God says so.
d) My Mom says so.

27

I'm older now, I have two sons of my own.
I've never told them about my incredible journey
and I've never shown them the magic *tallit*.
But we all share a great love for Passover,
the Seders, and our Jewish way of life.
It makes our lives together very special.

A key goal of Passover: to teach your children.
In the Torah, God says parents should tell their children
how God brought our ancestors out from Egypt and into
freedom. In fact, Haggadah literally means "telling."
Teaching our children ensures that the lessons of
Passover will live on forever with the Jewish people.

More Thoughts on Passover

How to have a truly great Passover Seder:
The key is to get everyone involved, regardless of age.
Take time to discuss the meaning of the customs and
rituals, and what it means to you personally or as a
family.   Don't just read the words... feel it! Get so
involved that you fulfill an important goal of Passover:
"to feel as if you had actually been freed from Egypt."

Tell Us Your Favorite Part Of Your Seder!

Maybe it's a song, a story or a special family tradition.
e-mail us at:
author@ruachbooks.com
We may even put it on our Web site: **www.ruachbooks.com**
to share with other kids and families!

Use a Haggadah that the whole family can enjoy.
We wrote **The *Really* Fun Family Haggadah**
for the entire family. Endorsed by the Deans of two
leading rabbinical schools, this illustrated Haggadah has
all of the Seder's 14 traditional steps, with easy-to-read
explanations and really fun multiple-choice questions.
You'll love it!

Answers to the Questions

Page 3
What's so important about the *tzitzit* of a *tallit*?
c) They're a symbol of God's 613 commandments.
In Hebrew, each letter of a word has a numerical value. If you add up the number value of each letter in the Hebrew word *tzitzit*, and add in the knots and fringes of the *tzitzit*, it adds up to 613, which is the total number of commandments in the Torah! By the way, the *tallit* given to Josh was used by his great-grandfather only on special occasions. His great-grandfather was buried in his regular *tallit*, which is according to Jewish custom.

Page 5
Which food reminds us of slaves making bricks?
d) Charoset (it looks like the mortar used for bricks)
Charoset is a mixture of foods, usually apples, nuts, wine and cinnamon, that we eat during the Passover Seder. It looks like the mortar used by our ancestors to keep the bricks stuck to each other. Believe me, making bricks was terrible – I know that first hand.

Page 6
How long were our ancestors slaves in Egypt?
d) 400 years
In the Torah, God told Abraham that his descendants would be slaves for 400 years, although some passages in the Torah quote different lengths of time. In any case, our ancestors were slaves in Egypt for hundreds of years, probably longer than the entire history of the United States! I was so sore after just one day of being a slave, can you imagine working that hard your entire life? This was truly a horrible time in our history and we should always be thankful to God for our freedom today.

Page 9
Many great leaders in the Bible were:
b) Shepherds
That's right, Moses, Jacob and King David were all shepherds! Moses would put his shepherd's skills to good use – he kept the Israelites together for forty years as they wandered through the desert. So, if you want to become a really great leader, first be a shepherd!

Page 10
When first told by God to help free the Israelites, Moses replied:
a) "Who me? Why would they listen to me?"
b) "What will I say when they ask Your name?"
At first, Moses didn't say yes to God's mission! But after some discussion, Moses finally agreed to help. Can you imagine God asking you to do something, and then giving God reasons why you shouldn't have been chosen to do it? I can't! (This question is from our Haggadah.)

Page 12
How did Pharaoh's magicians turn rods into snakes?
d) The rods were actually snakes, it wasn't magic at all.
Even today, "snake charmers" can turn a certain type of Egyptian cobra, called the *naje haje*, as stiff as a rod by pressing a special nerve! Then, when the stiff snake is thrown to the ground, the jolt enables it to recover and move as it usually does. I'd like to see that!

Page 14

What did Pharaoh's magicians call the third plague?

c) The finger of God

It took the third plague for Pharaoh's magicians to realize they were up against God, a force they couldn't match. Today, during the Passover Seder, as we say the Ten Plagues, some people dip a finger into their wine to remember that the plagues were the work of God, not a series of chance events.

Page 16

We still celebrate Jewish first-born males with a:

a) Pidyon Habben ceremony

b) Fast for the first born (during Erev Pesach)

These events are meaningful reminders that God spared our first born during the tenth plague in Egypt. Since I'm a first born, I'm especially happy about that!

Page 19

Midnight is important to Passover, it's when:

a) My Mom won't let me eat any more food.

b) The tenth plague struck the Egyptians.

c) We must have already eaten the Afikoman.

The *Afikoman* symbolizes the *Pesach* lamb sacrifice. Our ancestors ate the *Pesach* lamb during the Passover meal before midnight, since that's when the tenth plague struck. That's why, today, we eat the *Afikoman* before midnight. After eating the *Afikoman*, no one should eat any more food, so the taste stays with us through the night. Once again, Mom is right!

Page 21

Which sea did the Israelites cross?

c) The Sea of Reeds

Most people used to think the Israelites crossed at the Red Sea. But today, many experts believe the sea parted at the Sea of Reeds. The Torah calls the sea "yam suf," which literally means the Sea of Reeds. Fresh water seas have "suf" or reeds, salt water seas like the Red Sea do not. I guess we'll never really know!

Page 22

How did Moses part the sea and cave it back in?

d) He didn't – it was all the work of God.

From the plagues to the parting of the sea, it was all God's work, not Moses', who served as God's messenger. Before each miracle, God told Moses what to do (such as raise his rod or his arms), and God made it happen. That's why we should be so thankful to God for our freedom. Without God's help, we might still be slaves.

Page 24

The gold used to make the golden calf was:

d) Given to our ancestors by the Egyptians.

The Torah tells us that the Egyptians gave the Israelites gold as they left Egypt. Isn't it interesting how the riches we received from an idol-worshipping people were turned into an idol! Think about that!

Page 27

Why do we celebrate Passover?

a) It's the law!

c) God says so.

In the Torah, God commands the observance of Passover. Since God says to celebrate Passover in the Torah, and that's Jewish law, both a) and c) are correct! Of course, we'll give you credit if you also answered "d) Mom says so," since Mom is always right... right?

*In memory of my Mom, Barbara Stein, of blessed memory,
who inspired me to write and achieve my dreams.*

Ruach Publishing is dedicated to creating books and other content that spark the Jewish spirit (*ruach*) and inspire greater involvement in Judaism. *Josh Discovers Passover!* is intended to be the first of a series of *Josh Discovers!* books on the Jewish holidays and other major events. Our first book was *The Really Fun Family Haggadah*, published in 2000.

About the Author

The founder of Ruach Publishing, Larry Stein is deeply committed to inspiring families to greater involvement in Jewish life and learning. He is an active member of Congregation B'nai Tikvah, where he loves to chant Torah and Haftorah, and occasionally fill in to lead parts of services. *Josh Discovers Passover!* is Larry's second Jewish book, following *The Really Fun Family Haggadah*.

About the Illustrator

Illustrator and caricature artist Marlene K. Goodman owns MKG Graphics, a Wheeling, Illinois company providing creative and illustrative services. A former art teacher at Solomon Schechter, Marlene currently teaches art classes for adults and children. She is on the board of the Graphic Artists Guild of Chicago and is a past board member of the National Caricaturist Network. *Josh Discovers Passover!* is the sixth book she has illustrated. See more of Marlene's work at her Web site: www.mkggraphics.com

Acknowledgements

This book has been developed over several years, with tremendous guidance and inspiration by so many generous and knowledgeable leaders, especially: Rabbi Reuven Frankel, Rabbi Emeritus of Congregation B'nai Tikvah; Rabbi Dr. Martin S. Cohen of Congregation Eilat; Rabbi Allan Kensky, Rabbi William Lebeau and Dr. Steven Brown of The Jewish Theological Seminary; Jewish educators from Solomon Schechter and other organizations; and most importantly, my wife and two sons, my treasured and very loving consultants.

International Standard Book Number (ISBN): 0-9669910-1-X
Printed by Triangle Printers Inc., Skokie, Illinois